Author Focus

Develop Your Author Vision Statement and Laser-Focus Your Writing Career

Author Success Foundations Book 3

by

Christopher di Armani

ISBN-13: 978-1988938172

Editor: Nicolas Johnson

Published By:
Botanie Valley Productions Inc.
PO Box 507
Lytton, BC V0K 1Z0
http://BotanieValleyProductions.com

Dedication

This book is dedicated to my sweet and loving wife Lynda.

Without her unwavering support none of this would be possible.

Acknowledgments

Without the assistance of my editor, Nicolas Johnson, I can't imagine how this book would read. He tears my words apart from every conceivable angle, then offers thoughtful and constructive criticism on how best to fix the destruction at our feet. I thank God for Nicolas Johnson and his talents, daily.

#EditorsMatter

Feedback Loop

I also wish to express my heartfelt gratitude to the following individuals who took time from their own busy lives to critique this manuscript. Their willingness to assist a total stranger humbles me.

Kim Steadman (KimSteadman.com)
Sharilee Swaity (Facebook.com/Sharilee.Swaity)

Table of Contents

Chart Your Path to Success

A vision statement is your personal roadmap to success. A vision statement provides clarity and guides your decisions about your current and future courses of action. It reflects your core beliefs and values, and defines how to live your life to achieve your goals. It defines personal excellence for you.

As Lewis Carroll explained in *Alice's Adventures in Wonderland*, if you don't know where you want to go, the road you choose does not matter.

> *"Cheshire Puss,"* Alice began, rather timidly, as she did not know whether it would like the name: however, it only grinned a little wider. *"Would you tell me, please, which way I ought to go from here?"*
> *"That depends a good deal on where you want to get to,"* said the Cat.
> *"I don't much care where,"* said Alice.
> *"Then it doesn't matter which way you go."*

Your manuscript is not complete but you want to finish your book.

Publication Highway is the road you must travel, and your author vision statement is the road map to your destination.

Your author vision statement:

1. Combines every aspect your character.
2. Gives you focus.
3. Guides and simplifies your decisions.
4. Holds you accountable for your decisions and actions.
5. Acts as a unifying force for every action you take.
6. Motivates and inspires you to achieve your writing goals.

My heartfelt desire is for you to finish and publish your book, faster than you believe possible. My goal is to empower you to transform your dream into reality.

Your author vision statement is an extraordinary targeting mechanism to guide you to your ultimate destination - the end of Publication Highway.

The exercises ahead serve one purpose - to focus your mind on what you value most - your published book.

Writing is easy. Finishing your book is easy, too.

Focus. Be diligent. Apply self-discipline and determination. You already possess these qualities. This book would not appeal to you if you didn't.

Join me for the next 30 minutes and map the road to your personal success. Discover what you value most, not just in writing, but in your entire life. Isn't your ideal future worth the time?

Chapter 1

Foundations

Be Fearless

Your author vision statement must be:

1. Written down.
2. No more than two sentences long.
3. Written so clear a ten-year-old child can understand.
4. A statement you can (and will) recite from memory every morning to start your day.
5. The unique description of who you are and what core values drive you.
6. A unique statement to define your life's priorities.
7. A unique plan of action for you to achieve your goals.

You can (and should) set aside an entire day to focus on each step and complete the process.

The key?

Be fearless.

Don't be surprised if your preconceived notions smash against the rocks of reality. It happens. This process will force you to make decisions and follow through on your commitments.

When you complete your author vision statement you will gain new clarity about the highest vision you see for your life, but it all starts with a solid foundation.

Build a solid foundation for your writing.

Transform your mind into a powerful and focused ally for your future success and gain new clarity about how to achieve your goals.

Make two commitments right now. Promise me you will not start the exercises until you:

1. Read this book through in its entirety.

Take 30 minutes and read it through before you go to sleep at night. This allows your mind to absorb the scope of the task ahead. Your subconscious mind will start to solve the problem while you sleep.

2. Get a good night's sleep.

Read this book through a second time before you begin the exercises.

When you immerse yourself in this process with an honest and an open heart, you will uncover the three keys essential to your ideal future. Use those keys to construct the roadmap, the most direct path, to this future.

Shall we begin?

Chapter 2

Define Your Writing Dreams

What Do You Want To Write?

If you're like me, you want to write for different genres and a variety of audiences, with a little non-fiction tossed in for good measure. This runs counter to the advice of writing teachers and gurus everywhere. They insist you pick a single, tightly defined genre and stick to it, otherwise you will confuse your readers and lose your following.

I disagree. I believe readers are far smarter than that. When I discover an author I like, I'll read almost anything they publish, regardless of genre.

Let me give you an example.

About a year ago I stumbled across the Blood Bound vampire series by J.L. Myers. She is a talented writer who tells a great story and does it well. I devoured all three books in the series and reviewed them on Amazon.

When she published her psychological thriller Nerve Damage, a total departure from her previous work, I jumped at the opportunity to read it. Much to my delight, I found her thriller an even greater pleasure to read than her previous works, and I liked those a lot.

She is one of a handful of authors I will read, no matter the genre because she writes great books. I love reading good books by talented authors.

Readers are smart.

Treat them that way.

For the purposes of this exercise, I want you to figure out what you want to write and why, as clearly and specifically as possible.

Action Step

Do you want to write a fiction book? If so, what genre? More than one genre? Write them all down.

Do you want to write a self-help or other non-fiction book? If so, on what topic or topics?

List every project you want to write, in every genre, no matter how strange it appears. Take your time. There's no rush. It is more important to write a complete list than finish in two minutes without one.

When you're finished, rewrite the list in order of their importance to you and your overall life goals. It's easy to see what's not important, but I find it's more of a challenge to figure out what belongs at the top of my list. I suggest you build your list in reverse order, with your least favorite project at the top, then work your way down your original list.

Then cross off your least important goals. Cut away until five items remain.

Examine what remains. Resort your list again, if necessary. Then cross off your bottom three items. You may find the decision is easy from here, but if it's not, ask yourself one tough question.

If you knew you would die three days after you published your next book, which one of these two would you want as your legacy? That's your answer.

Write a detailed description of the project you want to write first.

Why Do You Want To Write It?

This is a difficult question to answer for many writers. It certainly is for me, especially with fiction books. I find it much easier with non-fiction projects.

For example, with my Author Success Foundations series, I want to teach writers how to write better, faster and publish more books every year.

With political non-fiction, I want to influence social policy or educate people about a specific government policy or politician's views.

These are all good and valid reasons. For fiction it's different, at least for me. The journey down Publication Highway is not the same, for starters. And while some of the reasons for writing non-fiction can apply, because the journey is so different, I find the reasons to write each story is too.

When I wrote my vampire script, I spent a about a year developing an interesting and compelling story. I loved the characters. I wanted to share them with the world. I also wanted to share something profound about the human experience and our search for redemption after we commit an atrocious and despicable act, the central theme of the movie.

For the Author Success Foundations series, there isn't a single reason. First, writing the series was a personal challenge, a dare to myself, to see if I could complete and publish 7 books in 90 days. This challenge is not my primary reason for writing the series though. In order to accomplish this goal in such a short time frame, I knew I needed to write about important issues. Important to me, if nobody else.

Action Step

What makes this project so important to you? Explain, in clear language, why you want to write it.

Write down every reason why this one tops your list. No rationale is off limits, even if it seems ridiculous right now. If you want to write the next Hollywood blockbuster, say so. This list is for your eyes only, so don't hold back. No matter how absurd a reason appears, if it enters your mind, write it down.

When you're done, see if you can find a common theme running through your answers. If you do, rewrite your explanation with an eye to grouping similar reasons together to build a strong and compelling statement.

What Do You Hope To Accomplish?

Different needs drive every author to write. A clear understanding of your personal motivation helps move you forward, even on the days you don't want to write.

When writing non-fiction for authors, my goal is to empower my readers in two ways.

First, to believe they can do more in less time and second, to encourage them to take concrete action to change their lives forever.

In fiction, the motivations may be different. The need to entertain your reader is obvious, but fiction is also a time-honored avenue for personal or social change.

Action Step

Define, in clear terms, what you hope to accomplish with this book. Do you want to change lives? Do you want to make your readers laugh or cry? Do you want to tell a beautiful story? Is there a specific goal this book will help you achieve? Write it all down.

What Are Your Strengths

Everyone excels at something, be it sports, driving, or cooking. The same is true for writing. We all excel at some parts of our craft, even if we are not so good at others.

For example, I love writing first drafts from a completed outline fast. Nothing pleases me more than pounding out 5,000-10,000 words every day during this process.

I'm also good at building detailed outlines, even if I don't particularly enjoy the process.

My writing is authentic because every word comes from my heart. That's important too.

I built systems so I self-edit my books in a methodical way that guarantees my professional editor receives a quality manuscript.

That's a pretty nice list of strengths. It's also pretty short. A list of my weaknesses would probably fill a dozen pages, but we'll save that exercise in self-flagellation for some the next section, as should you too.

Action Step

What are your core writing strengths?

Are you a good storyteller?

Does plot construction make your heart pound with joy?

Do the character flaws you gave your awesome hero excite you?

Do you write every day? Do you aim for a specific number of words every time you sit down to write?

List every ability you consider a writing strength. Sort it in order of what brings you the most joy. What three abilities top the list?

Acknowledge Your Weaknesses

Take a truckload of self-honesty and inject it with a gallon of pure caffeine. Guzzle it down, then work on the ugly bits ahead.

Nobody likes to admit their weaknesses, let alone write them down on paper. It's depressing, demoralizing and can lead to nasty hangovers after all the drinking is done.

Facing your weaknesses head-on is also necessary.

Be fearless.

Remember, nobody else will ever see this. In fact, I order you to burn the paper you write your answers on when your vision statement is complete. You need all of the pages until then. (Did he say *pages*?)

Here's a thought. Incorporate these traits into one of your characters. Make them pay for your weaknesses. Sounds fun, doesn't it?

Action Step

List all your weaknesses.

When you're finished, sort the list from your greatest weakness to your least. These are the areas you need to work on to further hone your skills.

When Do You Want To Complete Your Book?

In the previous steps, you defined what you want to write, why you want to write it and what you hope to accomplish with it. These are important pieces of your writing puzzle, but without a deadline they mean zilch.

A deadline empowers you with a sense of urgency.

Urgency drives you forward to take action.

Daily action transforms your unfinished manuscript into a published book.

In *Awaken Your Author Mindset* I gave you the formula I lovingly call Manuscript Math, a simple method to calculate how long it will take you to complete your book:

TWR / WPD = N

- ❑ TWR = Total Words Required to complete your book.
- ❑ WPD = How many words you Write Per Day.
- ❑ N = Number of days required to complete your book.

If your book should be 80,000 words and you write 500 words per day it will take you 160 days of writing to complete it.

Simple.

You shorten how long it takes to write your book by increasing how many words you write per day.

Again, simple.

I encourage you to push yourself, if only a little, when completing this action step. If you comfortably write 500 words per day, then base your deadline on writing 600 words each day.

The more you push yourself outside your comfort zone, the more you will accomplish, over time.

I didn't actually believe I could write, edit and publish seven books in 90 days when I set the goal but I wanted to push myself to see how many books I could finish in that time.

That's the thing about setting challenging goals and deadlines that force us out of our comfort zone. More often than not, we surprise ourselves by meeting those goals and deadlines.

In that respect, the human mind is truly remarkable. Once the goal is set, our subconscious mind simply gets on with the task to ensure we achieve it.

Action Step

When will you complete your manuscript?

Caveat: Your deadline must be within 12 months of today.

What Must Happen for You to Consider Your Writing as Successful?

Success is a different animal for every writer.

For some, it means financial independence.

For others, it means helping a specific number of people achieve a goal.

For many, it means freedom to deliver their message of hope to their target audience without constraint by outside forces.

Often, it is some combination of all these motivations.

For example, must you write a specific number of books this year? In your lifetime? Must you sell a specific number of books this year? Are you successful when a Hollywood producer options your story and turns it into a blockbuster movie?

Action Step

For you to say, "I'm a successful writer" what must happen? Be precise.

Chapter 3

Imagine The Possible

What Are Your Dreams?

What are your hopes and dreams?

Fling open the doors of possibility and list every answer to the question "If I could be, do and have anything, what would I dream?"

Don't restrict your answer to writing. Writing is only one part of your life. Include everything here since your final vision statement must reflect those dreams, too.

Action Step

What are your dreams for your life?

Money is No Obstacle. What do You do With Your Life?

Imagine today is Lottery Day and you won a cool $100 million, tax free. Money problems are for *other* people now, not you. Nothing is beyond reach. You're beyond the petty, mundane issues of everyday life.

This is a tough exercise.

We unconsciously tend to apply the limitations of our current life to our dreams, stifling and suffocating them in the process.

This is the time to breathe deep, exhale all your inhibitions about what is "possible" and swing for the stars. Think back to when you were a child. What was your craziest fantasy? Does it still apply?

My biggest desire to was to be a writer. The problem I faced was my internal negative self-talk that said, "You can't be writer until you have something to say." So I didn't write much.

Sure, I dabbled, but my internalized negativity made it difficult to write anything seriously until I was into my 30s. What a complete waste.

Don't be me. Be better than me.

Toss off your internal demons, plug your ears so you can't listen to their plaintive cries and see what's buried deep inside you. Then write it down and stare at it a while. You may be surprised at what you see.

Action Step

If your money problems disappeared, what would you do with your life?

Where would you live? Who would live there with you? What would you do all day? Close your eyes and picture, in your mind, your ideal life and all it entails.

Watch the movie in your mind and put it on paper. Describe your ideal life in clear and vivid terms.

If You Knew You Could Not Fail, What Would You Do?

Fear of failure is another terrible demon. It stops us from doing what we want to do most, for fear of what might happen. In this exercise bad things can't happen. Your only option is success. How big a success is up to you.

This is another swing for the fences exercise. Success is 100% guaranteed. How do you live your life in light of your new reality? Where do you go? How do you fill your days?

Action Step

Success is guaranteed. Describe your life under these new circumstances. Be specific.

Chapter 4

Honest Self-Evaluation

What was Most Effective For You Last Year?

Examine your past 12 months and honestly assess how you fared. Identify the tasks, personality traits and systems you used to succeed. What helped you achieve your goals? Your focus is on writing, but do not restrict your answers to those successes alone.

Action Step

Write down every tool, personality trait and system you used in the past year. Sort them in order of their ability to help you achieve success.

List Your Past Successes

Success leaves clues. In the previous section, you listed the systems, tools and personality traits you used to succeed. In this section, list every success you achieved using them.

Action Step

List your major successes from the past year, regardless of job type or area of life. What did you accomplish for your church, for your community, or for your family? Write it all down.

Examine your list for common themes and personality traits. What themes and traits do you find woven throughout your life?

List Your Recent Failures

We despise and ignore our failures and the causes for them. We focus on the one or two times we succeeded instead, despite those faults.

Action Step

If you need another truckload of self-honesty injected with pure caffeine, go for it. Take a big gulp and work on the next ugly bits.

Make an honest assessment of the actions you took over the past 12 months. Find those times where you did not succeed. It doesn't matter why. In every area of your life, list your failures over the past year. Beside each item, write down what you learned from the experience.

List Your Favorite Excuses

What is your go-to excuse when you fail?

- ❑ "I don't have time…"
- ❑ "It's not my fault."
- ❑ "Frank screwed up. If it wasn't for him, I could have made it."
- ❑ "I ran out of time. If I just had ten more minutes, I'd be finished."

This is my least favorite exercise, and for good reason. I **hate** my excuses.

However, personal responsibility is critical to success. When you accept full responsibility for the outcome of your actions, you learn from your mistakes. When you abdicate your responsibility you absolve yourself of accountability, another essential component of success.

How will you hold yourself accountable?

How will you be responsible for your actions, even when you fail to meet your objectives?

What truth will you use to combat your inclination to excuse your failures?

Action Item

What excuses do you use to justify your failure to write? List your excuses on the page, starting with your most-used rationalizations. Beside each one, explain why this excuse is groundless. What will you tell yourself instead?

Chapter 5

Your Personal Motivators

What Motivates You Best?

In a perfect world, our best motivators would also be positive ones, but the fear of a specific consequence can also drive you to succeed.

For example, if you fear bank foreclosure, this may inspire you to work hard to pay off your mortgage, even when you don't like your job.

Praise from others is also a powerful motivator.

Even silly things can be powerful motivators. For example, I love sour cream and onion potato chips. I also know they are terrible for me. Since I can't stop eating them and know decreeing I'll never eat them again is guaranteed to fail, I turned my love for these crunchy little pieces of heaven into a powerful motivator.

Whenever I publish a book in any format, I reward myself with a bag of chips. Publish the digital version of a book, get a back of chips. Publish a paperback version of the same book, get another bag of chips.

I honestly think the only reason I'm considering an audio-book version of this series is so I can eat another seven bags of these terrible treats.

The important takeaway here is that using potato chips as a reward is a powerful motivator for me. When making your list, put down everything that works for you, no matter how silly, absurd or outrageous it seems.

If it works, it's not silly, right?

Look back over the past two years and find those times you felt satisfied with your accomplishment. See if you can discern what factors inspired and drove you to achieve success then. Are those motivations still valid today?

Action Step

What do you fear? How does your fear motivate you?

What do you love? How does love motivate you?

Write down both positive and negative answers. When you're done, sort your list by the power it wields in your life.

What do you learn about yourself as a result of this exercise?

What Motivates You Least?

What attitudes and behaviors motivate you least? This is the reverse of the exercise you just completed.

For example, a Pomodoro Timer works for me.

It provides an imminent deadline and, even though I know it is 100% artificial, this deadline still inspires me to write. A friend of mine is the exact opposite. Deadlines don't motivate him. If I give him a deadline it won't get done. Ever.

Action Step

With these thoughts in mind, what sucks the motivation from your life? What causes you to shut down? This could be an action or an attitude in yourself or in others. Write them down.

What raises your hackles? What causes you to balk at the challenge in front of you?

How can you structure your life to avoid or minimize these motivational black holes?

Chapter 6

Your Core Values

Determine Your Core Values

Core values are your fundamental beliefs. These principles guide every decision you make in all areas of your life. They dictate your behavior, often unconsciously, and form your moral compass - how you define right and wrong.

Core values drive your behavior. They make you who you are. They are the unbreakable rules by which you live your life each day.

When you "feel bad" it is because you violate one or more of those core values. When you "feel good" it is because your actions are congruent with them.

There are no right or wrong answers, only truth and self-honesty.

Self-deception serves no purpose. When you lie to yourself about who you are, you guarantee failure, not success.

Action Step

This list of core values may be long, but don't let that intimidate you. Examine these core values and write down every one you believe guides your decisions and actions today.

Download the Core Values PDF Worksheet here:

http://ChristopherDiArmani.net/core-values-worksheet

CORE VALUES

Acceptance	Accomplishment	Achievement
Acknowledgement	Adaptability	Adventure
Affiliation	Ambition	Analytical
Appreciation	Approachability	Artfulness
Artistic Expression	Assertiveness	Assurance
Attentiveness	Authority	Autonomy
Availability	Balance	Beauty
Boldness	Bravery	Brilliance
Calmness	Care	Certainty
Challenge	Clarity	Cleverness
Comfort	Commitment	Community
Compassion	Competence	Competition
Complacency	Completion	Confidence
Connection	Consistency	Contemplative
Contentment	Contribution	Control
Conviction	Cooperation	Correctness
Courage	Creativity	Credibility
Cunning	Curiosity	Daring
Decisiveness	Delight	Dependability
Depth	Determination	Devotion
Directness	Discernment	Discipline
Discretion	Diversity	Duty
Education	Effectiveness	Emotional Health
Empathy	Encouragement	Enjoyment
Enthusiasm	Exactness	Excellence
Expediency	Experience	Expertise
Expressiveness	Facilitating	Fairness
Faith	Fame	Family-oriented
Fearlessness	Fidelity	Firmness
Fitness	Flexibility	Focus
Fortitude	Freedom	Friendly
Friendship	Frugality	Fulfilment
Fun	Generosity	Genuineness
Giving	Grace	Gratefulness
Gratitude	Growth	Guidance

Happiness	Hard working	Harmony
Health	Helpfulness	Heroism
High Earnings	Honest	Hospitality
Humility	Humor	Imagination
Impact	Independence	Industrious
Influence	Insightfulness	Inspiration
Integrity	Intelligence	Intimacy
Intuition	Inventiveness	Joy
Justice	Kindness	Knowledge
Leadership	Learning	Leisure
Logic	Love	Loyalty
Mastery	Maturity	Moderation
Nature	Openness	Optimism
Organization	Originality	Outgoing
Partnership	Passion	Peacefulness
Perfection	Perseverance	Persistence
Personal Growth	Personal Power	Persuasiveness
Playfulness	Pleasure	Positive
Predictability	Problem Solving	Professionalism
Prosperity	Punctuality	Purity
Recognition	Recreation	Relaxation
Reliability	Resilience	Resourcefulness
Respect	Responsibility	Risk-Taking
Security	Self-Control	Self-Discipline
Self-Expression	Self-Reliance	Self-Restraint
Service	Significance	Simplicity
Sincerity	Spiritual	Spirituality
Spontaneity	Stability	Status
Strength	Structure	Success
Sufficiency	Teamwork	Tenacious
Thoroughness	Time	Timeliness
Trust	Trustworthy	Truth
Understanding	Uniqueness	Unity
Usefulness	Variety	Vision
Warmth		

Find Your Seven Core Values

Take a few minutes to examine your list of core values. Sort them by priority, so those values you esteem most rank highest on your list.

Action Step

Cut your list down to the seven core values most important to you.

Cut Your List to Three

Take a few minutes to examine your list of seven core values. Sort them by priority again, if required.

Action Step

Cut your list to three.

These core values drive your actions and behaviors. They are the essence of who you are - qualities you value most in yourself and others. Reflect upon these values and examine your life for how they manifest in your thoughts, decisions and actions. Write down your discoveries.

Chapter 7

Write Your Own Obituary

If you Died Today, What Would be Your Biggest Regret?

Life is short. Nobody is guaranteed tomorrow, yet we behave as though time doesn't run out for us. *I'll do that tomorrow* is our mantra. It's also a lie, and one we repeat to ourselves every day.

Yesterday a 15-year-old boy died in the back of his parents' vehicle while they drove down the street. The fatal bullet, fired from a drug dealer's gun, snuffed out this boy's life. The drug dealer's intended target, rival gang members who shot at him from across the road, fled unharmed.

This boy and his family were, as the cliché says, in the wrong place at the wrong time. In a heartbeat, his young life ended - a horrible tragedy. When this 15-year-old boy woke up that fateful morning, he did not believe he would be dead before the sun went down. Even if you told him the bad news, he still wouldn't believe it.

The same is true for you and me. We are not promised tomorrow. Isn't it time our behavior reflected the fact today is a precious gift not to be squandered on useless and pointless tasks?

Action Step

If you died today, what would be your single biggest regret? What action will you take today to ensure you never face this dilemma?

Write Your Own Obituary

This exercise focuses on how you want to be remembered when you leave this world. Use how you want others to perceive your legacy to construct your road map to this destination. This also brings into focus how we're living right now. Is it congruent with your hopes and dreams? If not, what must you change so it is?

I want to be remembered as a man who inspired millions of other writers to follow their dreams down Publication Highway. If my words inspire a single person to get off the couch and publish a book, it's all worthwhile.

If you lived your ideal life, how would others describe you at your funeral?

Action Step

Your best friend will write your obituary and read it at your funeral. What would you want him or her to say? Be specific.

What Is Inscribed On Your Tombstone?

This is a fun yet challenging exercise because you are so limited by word count. You have, at most, a dozen words at your disposal. Never before has Hemingway's quip about getting the words right been so important.

Action Step

Write the inscription on your tombstone.

What One Change Can You Make
Today to Bring Your Vision to Life?

Your ideal life is described by your obituary and the inscription on your tombstone. What changes can you make in your life today to bring your vision closer to reality in the present?

Action Step

Define the one action you can take today to move you one step closer to the ideal vision of your life.

Chapter 8

How To Write Your Author Vision Statement

The Five Absolutes of a Compelling Vision Statement

Every question you answered until now delivered more clarity about your values and desires. You examined your strengths and weaknesses to better understand what motivates you. You now possess the raw information, the honest appraisal of self required to write your author vision statement.

1. It must be Clear

Your vision statement must reflect clarity of purpose. This is your guide for every future decision you make. The words you choose must power you through valleys of struggle and despair. Use action verbs to ensure your raw power is available when you need it most.

2. It must Compel you to excellence

Your vision statement must reflect the highest and best version of you, the one who accomplishes great things. Use words and phrases to inspire you and motivate you to excellence.

3. It must be Concise

Item 17 of Strunk and White's timeless manual for writers, *The Elements of Style,* is "Omit needless words."

"Vigorous writing is concise.

A sentence should contain no unnecessary words, a paragraph no unnecessary sentences, for the same reason a drawing should have no unnecessary lines and a machine no unnecessary parts."

What can I possibly add to E.B. White's brilliance?

A short, clear statement is always more powerful than a long-winded, rambling one.

4. It must be written in Present Tense

When written in present tense, your vision statement empowers you and makes you accountable for the standard you set. It puts integrity, the essential ingredient for success, atop the list of character traits you must develop.

Avoid passive language and future tense. Stay focused on the here and now, as you are in this moment. Couch statements in "I am" instead of "I will" or "I want to." Your vision statement should reflect the new reality you want to live now, even if you do not manifest it yet.

5. It must be Focused on the Long-Term

Your vision statement is for the months and years ahead. It defines the mark you want to leave on the world. It defines the imprint you want left on the lives of those you touch. It defines the legacy you want to leave when you're gone. Your statement should draw others into your vision, too.

Your First Draft

The purpose of a first draft is to vomit words on the page. Nothing more, nothing less.

Yes, this applies to your author vision statement, too.

You win no points for style.

Don't start big - start HUGE.

Write down every character trait you value. Write down every skill you possess, every goal you hope to achieve.

Dump it all out on the page.

Shine the spotlight of honesty and integrity upon it and discover the true vision for your life.

Action Step

Write down everything you discovered is important to you, why it is important and what you want to do to achieve it. Don't worry about order at this stage. We'll address priorities when you're done.

Edit Your First Draft

Rewriting is where the magic happens. This is true for both epic novels and vision statements.

Take what you wrote on the previous page and sort it. Present it in a sensible order. Hack and slash away everything you don't hold in the highest esteem. Murder any darlings you left on the page.

If this takes time, don't worry. If you must stop and return to it tomorrow, no problem, but set an appointment with yourself to complete this step and **keep the appointment.**

Action Step

Cut your author vision statement down to a single paragraph. (*Yes, one paragraph can fill an entire page.*)

Your Final Draft

As discussed earlier, your author vision statement must be:
1. Written down.
2. No more than two sentences long.
3. Written so clear a ten-year-old child can understand.
4. A statement you can (and will) recite from memory every morning to start your day.
5. The unique description of who you are and what core values drive you.
6. A unique statement to define your life's priorities.
7. A unique plan of action to achieve your goals.

The final, polished draft of your author vision statement should be 100 words, at most. If you can write it in 50, even better.

Points are for brevity, clarity of purpose, motivation and action.

Action Step

Take the paragraph you wrote in the previous step and rewrite it into your final Author Vision Statement.

Victory!

I congratulate you for your courage and tenacity. You finished an exercise most human beings will never even attempt.

This is a massive accomplishment, so pat yourself on the back.

You earned it!

Step back and admire your vision for your ideal future, then perform every task required to breathe life into your dream until it becomes your reality.

Then share your vision with the world.

Chapter 9

Power Points

Refining Your Vision Statement Never Ends

Your Author Vision Statement is, in the truest sense, a living document. You must revisit and revise it over time.

The Bible, in Luke 14, verse 28, exhorts us to "count the cost."

> *For which of you, intending to build a tower, does not sit down first and count the cost, whether he has enough to finish it; lest, after he has laid the foundation, and is not able to finish, all who see it begin to mock him, saying, 'This man began to build and was not able to finish.'*

To achieve your ideal life you must count the cost of achievement, then work hard every day to pay the price. You must build your personal tower of success. You must count the full cost of your published book in time, talent, skill development and treasure, and pay this price daily until you achieve your goal.

There is no other way. If an easier path existed, everyone would write and publish a book. They don't. You will.

Action Proves Motivation

Action is proof of your motivation to succeed.

To write a book, you must take action. Pretty simple, right?

The following steps help you take action *today*.

Identify One Strength You Can Use Today

You created a list of your strengths in Chapter 2. Examine this list and identify your primary strength. Next, identify every way you can put this strength to work in your life today. How can you modify your writing routine to use your primary strength on a more regular basis?

Identify Another Strength You Can Use Today

From the same list, identify one more strength you can put to work today, and continue to do more often, to support your personal sense of achievement.

Identify One Thing You Can Do Today to Bring You More Joy

Identify the one skill you excel at, the one skill you love doing most that you can use today to draw more joy into your life.

Make the commitment to use this skill more often, every day, if possible. The more joy you experience in life, the happier you are. The happier you are, the more productive you become.

What a wonderful and self-fulfilling cycle. Put it to work for you today.

What is the one skill you can use today, and use with greater frequency in the future, to bring more joy to your life?

The Path to Success is Written on Paper

Research by Dr. Gail Matthews[1] at the Dominican University of California confirmed the results of a never-performed, but oft-cited Harvard or Yale study on the power of written goals. The mythical study claimed only 3% of the graduating class wrote down their goals and 20 years later out-earned their classmates by over ten times.

While not quite so earth-shattering as multiplied earning power, Dr. Matthews' study confirms when you write down your goals you are more liable to follow through and achieve them.

When you take one simple action and write down your goals, you increase your likelihood to follow through on your commitment and take the actions necessary to achieve your goals.

Pretty simple, right? Obvious, even, yet so many people do not write down their goals. They decrease their chances for success out of sheer laziness. That's crazy. If you prefer to work through these exercises on a pre-designed form, please download your free digital copy of the Author Vision Statement Workbook from:

http://ChristopherDiArmani.net/author-vision-statement-workbook

The Road to Success Continues: How to Become a Prolific Author

Success matters. The road you travel to achieve success matters even more.

A daily routine makes you a more prolific writer. Your daily routine is also the last piece of the puzzle to create a life focused on one goal - your published book.

Becoming an unstoppable writer is the natural outflow of fulfilling your core needs, but you still require structure to build your habits upon to guarantee your success.

A daily routine, tailored to the wants, needs and commitments of your life, is essential to the fastest and shortest journey down Publication Highway.

Every writer's life is different. Your ideal daily writing routine is different than mine, and for good reason. You aren't me. Our lives differ, maybe a little, maybe by orders of magnitude. Who knows? Who cares? Our differences do not matter - our similarities do.

Prolific Author - The Step-by-Step Guide to Write More Words in Less Time and Finish Your Book Fast uncovers those similarities, but only when you take action, when you complete the exercises with complete honesty.

Learn how to create a system, a daily writing routine, designed to push you forward to your goal. Follow this system and I guarantee you will finish your book and publish it, too.

Available from your favorite online book retailers today.

For more information, visit:

https://ChristopherDiArmani.net/prolific-author

One Last Thing!

First, thank you for reading this book!

If you enjoyed this book and found it informative (and even if you did not) I would be grateful if you would post an honest review on Amazon and/or Goodreads. Every review helps this book find more readers, the lifeblood of any author.

http://ChristopherDiArmani.net/review-author-vision-amazon

http://ChristopherDiArmani.net/review-author-vision-goodreads

Your support in the form of an honest review really does make a difference. Reviews help authors sell more books and I read every one as part of my efforts to make my books even better.

I would also be grateful if you shared a link to this book on your social media accounts.

If, for some reason, you did not like this book or didn't get what you expected out of it please tell me directly. I will use your constructive criticism to fix any flaws in my book so it better meets your expectations. Please contact me here:

https://ChristopherDiArmani.net/Contact

Thank you so much for your support, feedback and your honest reviews.

Sincerely,

Christopher di Armani

Author Extraordinare

http://ChristopherDiArmani.net

About Christopher di Armani

"Author Extraordinaire"

Christopher di Armani is an Amazon bestselling author and the creator of Author Success Foundations.

This 7-book series teaches authors at any level how to develop the mindset, daily routines and work habits necessary to unleash their creativity and get their books published.

He has published 16 books and produced 4 documentary films on topics ranging from the craft of writing to civil liberties and politics.

Download your free introduction to the Author Success Foundations series at

https://ChristopherDiArmani.net/AuthorSuccessFoundations

Books by Christopher

Awaken Your Author Mindset: Finish Writing Your Book Fast (Author Success Foundations 1)

https://ChristopherDiArmani.net/author-mindset

https://ChristopherDiArmani.net/author-mindset-workbook

Learn how to develop your bullet-proof Author Mindset and create a system guaranteed to deliver success and to build the habits required to work this system every single day.

The choice is yours. If you continue to do what you've always done you'll just get what you already have, an unfinished manuscript and all the disappointment, discarded dreams and self-loathing you can handle.

You will never finish your book.

Now, imagine the possible...

Allow me to be your guide to help you construct a mindset, a solid foundation to complete your manuscript so published becomes, not just possible, but inevitable. This is the power of the Author Mindset.

Design Your Morning Routine: Jump-Start Your Writing Success (Author Success Foundations Book 2)

https://ChristopherDiArmani.net/morning-routine

https://ChristopherDiArmani.net/morning-routine-workbook

There is no magic to writing a book. None. You take action, every single day, until your book is finished. You plan, schedule and execute the plan. You write.

If you are serious about finishing your manuscript, grab your notebook, a pen, and a cup of your favorite beverage, and join me at the kitchen table. We'll chat about habits, willpower and self-discipline. We'll discuss how the mind functions, what makes a habit stick, and how our willpower fades throughout the day. We'll talk about concrete steps to improve your self-discipline.

Then I'll ask you to complete a series of exercises. These exercises reveal, at a deep level, what's important to you - what you value most in life. This clarity of purpose allows you to create a morning routine designed to jump-start your daily writing output.

Author Focus: Develop Your Author Vision Statement and Laser-Focus Your Writing Career (Author Success Foundations Book 3)

https://ChristopherDiArmani.net/author-focus

https://ChristopherDiArmani.net/author-focus-workbook

Writing is easy. Finishing your book is easy, too.

Focus. Be diligent. Apply self-discipline and determination.

You already possess these qualities. This book would not appeal to you if you didn't.

Your author vision statement is an extraordinary targeting mechanism to guide you to your ultimate destination - the end of Publication Highway.

The exercises ahead serve one purpose - to focus your mind on what you value most - your published book.

Join me and map your personal journey down Publication Highway. Discover what you value most, not just in writing, but in your entire life.

Isn't your ideal future worth the time?

Prolific Author: The Step-by-Step Guide to Write More Words in Less Time and Finish Your Book Fast (Author Success Foundations 4)

https://ChristopherDiArmani.net/prolific-author

https://ChristopherDiArmani.net/prolific-author-workbook

The key to unlock your drive to succeed is knowing why you write. When you understand how your desire to write fulfills your core needs, you transform writing from a chore to be dreaded into the vision you were born to fulfill. Time set aside to write becomes as critical to your life as the food you eat and the water you drink.

If we believe success does not matter, neither does the road we travel to get there.

Success matters. The road you travel to achieve success matters more.

Your daily writing routine is the last piece of the puzzle to build a life focused on accomplishing your goal - a finished and published book.

Done is Better than Perfect: 7 Keys to Finish Writing Your Book Fast (Author Success Foundations 5)

https://ChristopherDiArmani.net/done-better-perfect

Give Up Your Perfectionism and Publish Your Book

The three fundamental truths of writing are:

1. Your book will never be perfect.

2. You cannot publish what you do not complete.

3. Done is better than perfect.

Learn how to finish your book easier, faster and better than you ever thought possible when you apply the Seven Keys of Writing Success.

Become Unstoppable: 7 Habits of Highly Successful Authors (Author Success Foundations Book 6)

https://ChristopherDiArmani.net/become-unstoppable

Success leaves clues.

Figure out what successful authors did to advance their careers, then do what they did. It's the most effective course of action. Simple concept, but we must do the work. You know, the hard part.

In the pages ahead I discuss how each habit works, as well as the lies we tell ourselves to rationalize our lack of forward progress. Finally, I shine the light of truth on the lies we tell ourselves and watch as they scurry away like little cockroaches.

Apply these principles to your life and you'll achieve their success. It's inevitable. All it takes is a pinch of perseverance, a dash of focus, and two cups of hard work.

I Don't Have Time To Write And Other Lies Writers Tell Themselves (Author Success Foundations Book 7)

https://ChristopherDiArmani.net/no-time-to-write

Stop Lying To Yourself.

In this installment of the Author Success Foundations series, I dissect seven lies writers tell ourselves and shine the light of truth upon each one.

Every falsehood obscures a truth we refuse to confront. The job of a writer, any writer, is to face our fears head on, protected by the body armor of honesty and integrity. Only then does the brilliance we etch on the page shine bright for the world to see.

Each delusion corrodes holes in our armor, holes the insidious demons of worry, self-doubt, procrastination and perfectionism slip through to poison us.

The Author Success Foundations series provides the tools and materials to patch those holes, to reinforce and strengthen our armor. The day of battle is here, and we must march ever forward. If we stop, even for a moment, our words shrink under the oppressive heat of our fears and we fail.

Step inside. Face your fears. Show these pathetic demons you cannot be cowed. Own your internal dialog and reshape it into a powerful engine, then use that power to drive down Publication Highway.

The Simple 3-Step Secret to Slaughter Writer's Block And Vanquish it Forever

https://ChristopherDiArmani.net/Writers-Block-Book

There is no more perfect Hell than one where I cannot write. You know that terror, too, don't you? That sense your last remaining creative spark abandoned you some time back. It's sickening.

Let me show you how to extricate yourself from that "perfect Hell" permanently.

TOP SECRET - Inspiration, Motivation and Encouragement - 701 Essential Quotes for Writers

https://ChristopherDiArmani.net/Top-Secret-Quotes

This compilation of 701 quotes delivers inspiration, motivation and encouragement on 39 aspects of writing and the writing life.

You will discover quotes to make you laugh and quotes to make you cry. Some are familiar, like old friends. Others you will meet for the first time. All have a common theme: The Writing Life.

When you need it most, you will find words of encouragement here.

Filming Police is Legal - How to Hold Police Accountable While Staying Out of Jail

I write about police issues regularly. I highlight good cops when I can, but I focus on the problems in our police forces with honesty, integrity and abuse. Every time news breaks about police seizing another citizen's camera or cell phone I receive the same question.

Christopher, is it legal to film police?

The unequivocal answer is a court-affirmed YES. It is legal to film police in every state in the United States of America and in every single province and territory of Canada. That YES comes with specific caveats for the audio portion of a recording depending upon your jurisdiction, and it is critical you know those caveats.

The purpose of this book is to educate mere citizens and police forces alike about the legality of the right of citizens to film police, along with an examination of the legal history supporting our legal right to do so.

https://ChristopherDiArmani.net/Filming-Police

Justin Trudeau - 47 Character-Revealing Quotes from Canada's 23rd Prime Minister and What They Mean for You

On October 19, 2015 Canadians elected their 23rd Prime Minister based on good looks, nice hair and a famous name.

They voted for style over substance.

Our 23rd Prime Minister's entire leadership experience consisted of teaching snowboarding lessons and high school drama. His management experience consisted of administering his trust fund and his ego.

Not a single thought was given to what he stood for, what his party stood for, or what he would actually do once elected to the highest office in the land. That bothered me. That bothered me so much I began to research his much-publicized missteps and that in turn revealed a disturbing pattern within Trudeau's numerous faux pas. That pattern is the focus of this book.

https://ChristopherDiArmani.net/Justin-Trudeau-Book-1

From Refugee to Cabinet Minister: Maryam Monsef's Meteoric Rise to Power and her Spectacular Fall From Grace

Maryam Monsef is the ultimate immigrant success story. She could not speak English when she arrived in Canada at age eleven. Two decades later she became Canada's first Muslim Cabinet Minister.

Maryam Monsef's story begins with her mother, a young Afghan widow who fled Afghanistan for Canada with her three young daughters in 1995. That widow spoke English but her three daughters did not. They brought something far more valuable to Canada: the unshakeable belief they could accomplish anything they wanted, so long as they worked hard.

It's no accident her belief in herself led Maryam Monsef to a Cabinet post. She worked hard to learn English and graduated from Trent University, an impossible accomplishment in her native Afghanistan.

Maryam Monsef became the unwitting scapegoat for Trudeau's broken promise on electoral reform, a promise he knew he would break by May 2016. Her birthplace controversy, her attempts to discredit and insult her electoral reform committee, combined with the Prime Minister's betrayal of her trust, sounded the death knell of her political career.

This, then, is the story of one young woman's meteoric rise to political power. It is also the story of that young woman's undoing at the hands of a narcissistic and self-serving celebrity feminist, Justin Trudeau.

https://ChristopherDiArmani.net/Maryam-Monsef-Book

Endnotes

1   Matthews, Dr. Gail. "Study demonstrates that writing goals enhances goal achievement." Dominican University of California, Jan. 5, 2017, https://www.dominican.edu/dominicannews/study-demon-strates-that-writing-goals-enhances-goal-achievement. Accessed: Jan. 18, 2018.

www.ingramcontent.com/pod-product-compliance
Lightning Source LLC
LaVergne TN
LVHW052039080426
835513LV00018B/2391